Timeless Child Arts

Pen & Pencil Play - Into the Zone

Zany Variations

Designed by Toni the Doodler

ISBN:
ISBN-13: 978-1530563456
ISBN-10: 1530563453

DEDICATION

I dedicate this to my children who have inspired me to face adversity bravely and with determination and who have forgiven me whenever I have not managed to meet my own expectations, loving me unconditionally as I do them. Though they are always the cause of my greatest fears, they are also and always will be the cause of my greatest joys and hopes and undeniably my greatest ever achievements.

You make me so very proud to be your Mum

ACKNOWLEDGMENTS

I have a few friendships that are decades in existence and some that formed as a result of starting out as my clients, some from my love of dancing and some more recent ones who simply started as neighbours. I am so lucky to have these friendships and I treasure them every day. We bonded through shared suffering in many instances and we have been there for each other through trials large and small. This is the first of the books that will be my way to say thank you so much for standing by me, for sharing your heart and soul with me, for giving me some of the happiest moments in my life and for believing. I hope you find something in these pages that will help you be in the zone when you need it most.

In this first volume I have tried to add different styles of pictures, offering opportunities to colour something quickly and get that buzz of achievement, or spend hours filling something in that will look completely different once colour is added and life is breathed into it. There are also pictures that offer the perfect opportunity to shade and add depth. Most of them are feint lines so that what shows up is your coloring artistry, not bold lines in the design and I've also left a bit of room at the gutter (iner margin) in case there's any that you'd rather cut out and frame etc. I would love some feedback on what you liked most and an idea of the reasons why. Have fun, Toni

Timeless Child is the brand name of the works completed by Toni the Doodler. Toni was born in London in 1963 and is an artist and a poet, with lengthy interruptions to her creative existence while doing 'proper jobs' as advised by her elders and betters. Now returning to art in its many forms, she feels more herself when creating her artwork from painting and drawing (pet portraits a speciality) through colouring books to glass painting and also her poetry which ranges from greetings, through passionate and loving, to dark and disturbed. She creates coloring books and plans a series of volumes of her poetry.

Based in the UK, Toni has four adult children, 2 boys and 2 girls, sharing her home with her youngest son and their dogs who can generally be found by her side.

Find her on Facebook and upload your coloured pages:
http://www.facebook.com/Toni.the.Doodler

Her website is:
http://timelesschildarts.wix.com/toni-the-doodler